Instructions on page 18

for the ceremony, planning the celebration, booking the honeymoon… and the list goes on.

This is where your opportunity as a bridesmaid comes in. Your responsibility is to support and assist the happy bride before, during, and after the ceremony so the wedding can be the best day of her life.

Here is a checklist of a few of the things you can do to assist the bride.

• Help with planning the colors… suggesting what might be sentimental or appropriate, and helping carry these through the entire theme.

• Assist with the invitations… preparing the list, creating the invitations, addressing the envelopes, and delivering them to the post office.

Tip: you'll find a great collection of quick and clever wedding invitations, cards and more right in this book.

• Locate appropriate bridesmaid dresses.

• Assist in planning the florals.

• Suggest great gifts. You will find a wonderful collection of simple beaded jewelry in this book.

• Keep the bride company, provide moral support and help make her day perfect.

We wish you an enjoyable bridesmaid, friendship and wedding experience… Happy Wedding!

Index of Projects

Bridesmaids ... Help for the Bride

There is so much more to being a bridesmaid than walking down the aisle. This is when your best friend needs you the most. Help the bride and groom have an experience of a lifetime. Get Creative! The bride is worried about details. Start a planner to keep up with the bride's duties as well as your own.

Bridesmaids Are the Bride's Sanity. You must be on call 24 hours a day. Let the bride know you will be there, ready to assist and support her whenever she needs you. Brides really need a friend to help calm them down in moments of panic. Listen, remember and make every wish come true.

Invitations: Coordinate with the bride and determine when the invitations are to be sent. Communicate with other bridesmaids to find out when to help with writing addresses, stuffing envelopes and putting on stamps.

Cameras: Collect disposable cameras at night's end and get them developed.

Wedding Gown: Take her gown to the cleaners after the wedding. Make sure one of the groomsmen assumes responsibility for the groom's tuxedo.

As a bridesmaid, it is your duty to help the bride with the wedding. After all, you agreed to be a bridesmaid because the bride means a great deal to you. Why not let her know how much you care? Here are some extra-special, go-the-distance ways to show her how happy you are to be part of the wedding:

Wedding Countdown: Check on your bride every other day. Brides need to feel they have help planning the wedding. Sometimes they just need to talk.

Pamper the Bride. Take her to get her nails done, get a massage, or just to enjoy a nice coffee break. Give her a gift certificate to her local spa. With all the expenses of a wedding, this is something she could really use.

Get the Girls! (Bridesmaid) Take a weekend trip to a bed and breakfast or just share a relaxing night together.

Start a Scrapbook. To make this process easier, ask all the bridesmaids to contribute. You will want to start right away. Document every event: Wedding dress shopping, showers, dinners, etc. Photos depicting "before Mr. Right" provide a nice place to start. Follow up with meeting Mr. Right. Ask for pictures from the proposal.

A Popular Rehearsal Surprise is a slide show of the bride and groom growing up and then meeting each other. It will bring tears from both sides.

What Does a Bridesmaid Pay for? As a bridesmaid you will need to pay for your dress and accessories. You will also be responsible for the shower location and decorations. The bachelorette party is a big one. This is her last night out before getting married.

Large Tux Card

Write, print or rubber stamp 'Congratulations' on White cardstock.

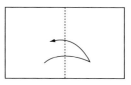 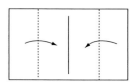

1. Cut Black and White cardstock 4" x 10". Fold in half vertically, unfold.

2. Fold left and right sides in half to meet center fold line.

3. For coat, fold top right center corner diagonally out to right side. Repeat on left side. Tuck white shirt inside tux coat.

4. For tux shirt, fold top right center corner diagonally out to the right to meet the edge of the tux lapel. Repeat on left side.

5. Pierce a small hole through lapel. Insert and glue a small silk rose in hole on lapel.

Folded Pants

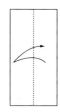 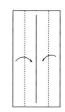

1. Cut a 3" x 6" rectangle of paper. With white side up, fold in half lengthwise. Crease and unfold.

2. Fold each half in half lengthwise to meet at center.

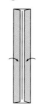 

3. Fold in half again along existing crease.

4. Fold diagonally in half to make pants.

5. Slide pants into opening at bottom of shirt.

Small Tux Card

MATERIALS: Cardstock (2" x 4" White; Black: 5½" x 8½", 2" x 4") • 4" x 5" White translucent Vellum • Tiny Pink ribbon rose • Decorative scissors

INSTRUCTIONS:
Fold large Black cardstock to 4¼" x 5½" card. • Print words on vellum. Trim vellum edges with scissors, glue to card.

Tux Shirt: Fold 2" White cardstock edges to meet at center. Fold down top corners to make collar. • **Tux Jacket:** Fold 2" edges of Black cardstock to almost meet at center. Fold short edges at an angle to make lapels. • Place White shirt inside of Black jacket. Glue to center. • Glue a rose to lapel.

Folded Shirt

Size: 2:1 ratio

 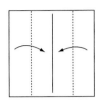

1. Cut a 3" x 3" square of paper. Fold square in half, unfold.

2. Fold each half in half again to meet at center.

3. To find center, fold in half top to bottom, then unfold.

 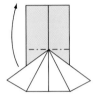

4. Fold bottom inside right and left corners out.

5. Fold bottom half back to meet top edge.

6. Fold top center right and left corners down to form collar.

7. Fold tip of shoulders back to round them off.

8. Optional: Fold sides diagonally to form taper.

9. Finished shirt.

Pleated Skirt

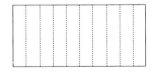

1. Cut a 2" x 6" strip of paper. To make pleats the same size and to fold accurately, lightly draw guidelines on the back of paper with a pencil and ruler.

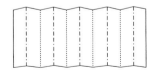

2. Fold paper back and forth to crease along each line.

3. Shape accordion folds into a skirt. Stretch lower end for fullness and upper end to match width of shirt.

Fabulous Folded Wedding Cards

Make truly unique wedding gift cards and invitations. Fold black and white Vellum papers and cardstock into elegant invitations and 'Thank You' notes for friends and attendants.

Bride & Groom Clothes

MATERIALS:

Groom: Cardstock (4" x 6" White; Black: 6½" x 11", 4" x 6") • Small silk rose • Adhesive

Bride: White cardstock (7½" x 10", 5" x 5") • Adhesive

INSTRUCTIONS:

For Groom:

Fold 4" x 6" White and Black cardstock following the Large Tux Card diagram. • Tuck White folded cardstock inside of Black cardstock to make shirt and coat. • Fold 6½" x 11" Black cardstock following the Folded Pants diagram. • Position pants under coat. Secure with glue. • Add rose.

For Bride:

Accordion fold 7½" x 10" White cardstock. • Glue to a White cardstock triangle base to hold fan position to desired fullness. • Fold 5" x 5" White cardstock following Shirt diagram. Glue shirt over top edge of accordion skirt.

Embroidery on Paper

Wedding invitations and cards are filled with glowing golden accents. These wedding day memorabilia are perfect little treasures that any bridesmaid can make for the bride... and they will become family heirlooms.

Gold and ivory are a combination to make any wedding photo or card shine with the love that fills an unforgettable day.

  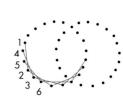

BASIC STEPS
Pattern. Photocopy the desired pattern. Attach to open card with artist's medium sticky masking tape.
Piercing.
Place on a piercing pad. Pierce card with a fine tool holding tool vertically. Check pattern against light for any unpierced holes. Remove pattern.

Embroidery. Select and cut 36" of thread. Double thread for an attractive effect. Insert needle from back of card leaving a 1½" tail. Secure tail with tape outside the pierced holes. When ending thread, secure in the same manner.
Tip: Insert the needle in one hole at a time to prevent paper tears.

Finish. Glue coordinating cardstock on the back of design to hide stitching.
Tips:
• The needle should always be thinner than the piercing tool. Check by inserting the needle in a pierced hole.
• Dip end of thread in glue to prevent fraying. Allow to dry.

BASIC MATERIALS:
Basic Supplies: Metallic Gold thread • Thin sewing needle • White cardstock or cards • Piercing tools (coarse and fine) or a large pin • Foam piercing pad • Glue stick

Gift Tag
MATERIALS: Cream cardstock (3" x 4½", 2½" x 4") • 2¾" x 4¼" Gold metallic paper • Fine-tip marker • 12" of 3mm strung pearls • ¼" hole punch
INSTRUCTIONS:
Follow Gift Tag pattern. On 2½" x 4" cardstock, pierce a hole at A with a coarse tool and other holes with a fine piercing tool. • Insert needle at A and pull thread to each hole as indicated. • Go across back to A and pull thread firmly. • Trim cardstock and paper pieces to tag shape. • Stack and glue pieces. • Write name with pen. • Punch a hole at the top and tie pearls through hole.

'For You' Gift Card
MATERIALS: 2½" x 4½" Cream folded card • 2½" x 4½" Gold metallic paper • ⅜" Gold letter stickers • Scallop brass embossing stencil • Stylus
INSTRUCTIONS:
On front of card, pierce holes with fine piercing tool. • Emboss lower edge and cut along scallops. • Use Wedding Rings pattern. Insert needle up at 1 and pull thread down at 2. Go up at 3 and pull thread down at 4. Repeat until each ring is complete. • Add letter stickers. Glue Gold paper inside card.

'Two Shall Become One Card
MATERIALS: Cream cardstock (1½" x 2¼", 2¼" x 3") • 5" square Cream folded card • 2" x 2¾" Gold metallic paper • ⅜" Gold letter stickers • Wavy edge scissors
INSTRUCTIONS:
Use Wedding Rings pattern. On 1½" x 2¼" cardstock, pierce holes with fine piercing tool. • Insert needle up at 1 and pull thread down at 2. Go up at 3 and pull thread down at 4. Repeat until each ring is complete. • Add letter stickers to front of card. • Trim Gold paper with wavy edge scissors. • Stack and glue paper and cardstock pieces.

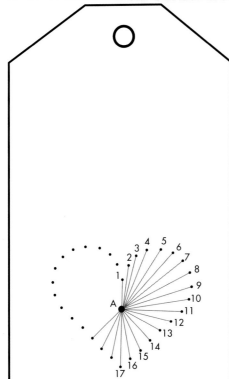

Square Heart Card

MATERIALS: 4⅞" square Cream cardstock for liner, 5" square Cream folded card • Scallop brass embossing stencil • Stylus

INSTRUCTIONS:

In center of 5" square, follow pattern to pierce holes. • Emboss scallop frame around heart. • Insert needle up at 1 and pull thread down at 2. Go up at 3, pull thread down at 4. Repeat until heart is complete. • Follow border pattern to pierce holes at A with coarse piercing tool. Insert needle from back at A and pull thread to holes. At corners repeat from B. • Glue liner to cover back of embroidery.

Lace Edge Card

MATERIALS: 3⅞" x 5⅝" Cream cardstock for liner, 4" x 5¾" Cream folded card • 5¾" Cream 1" flat lace • 5¾" of 3mm strung pearls • ½" Gold letter stickers • Gem-Tac

INSTRUCTIONS:

On front of card, pierce holes. • Insert needle up at 1 and pull thread down at 2. Go up at 3 and pull thread down at 4. Repeat until one side of heart is complete. • Repeat to make other side. • Embroider the second heart. • Glue liner to cover back of embroidery. • Adhere lace and pearls along edge of card with Gem-Tac.

Gift Tag

MATERIALS: Cream cardstock squares (2"; 3") • 2½" square Gold metallic paper • Decorative scissors

INSTRUCTIONS:

On a 2" square, pierce 8 center holes with a coarse tool and other holes with a fine tool. • Insert needle at A and pull thread to holes. • Go across back to A. Repeat from each large hole. • Trim Gold metallic paper with decorative scissors. • Stack and glue cardstock and paper.

Heart in Diamond Card

MATERIALS: Cream cardstock squares (4⅞" for liner, 2¾") • 5" Cream square folded card • 3¼" square of Gold metallic paper • Decorative scissors

INSTRUCTIONS:

On a 2¾" square, pierce a hole at A with a coarse tool and other holes with a fine tool. • Insert needle at A and pull thread to each hole as indicated. Go across back to A and pull thread firmly. • For corners on card, pierce holes at A with a coarse tool and other holes with a fine tool. • Insert needle from back at A and pull thread to holes. • Trim Gold paper with decorative scissors. • Stack and glue embroidered square and paper. Cover embroidery with liner.

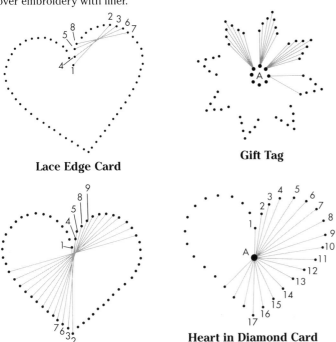

Lace Edge Card

Gift Tag

Heart in Diamond Card

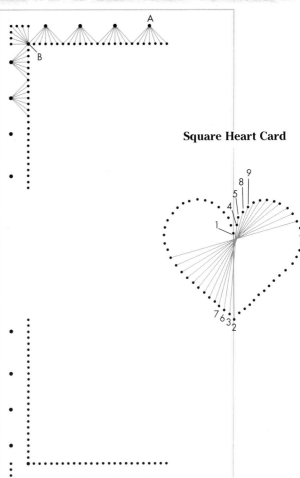

Square Heart Card

Wedding Mini-Clothing

Soft is the feeling of the clothes in this wedding party. Use the darling patterns to make miniature clothing to adorn cards, favors, scrapbook pages and gifts.

Basic Instructions
1. Trace and cut out a paper pattern.
2. Pin pattern to felt. Cut out felt shape.
3. Use thread or 2 ply floss to sew a Running stitch around the edge.
4. Sew or glue embellishments in place.

Tuxedo Jacket
MATERIALS: Felt (3" x 4" Black, 1" x 2" White) • 3 Black ¼" buttons • *DMC* Gray floss •

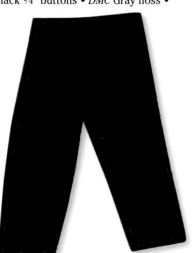

Tuxedo Pants
MATERIALS: 3" x 3" Black felt • *DMC* Gray floss

Ring Bearer Pillow
MATERIALS: White felt squares (1" and 2") • 4" White ⅛" ribbon • 2 small jump rings • 1 Crystal bicone bead • *DMC* White floss

Wedding Dress
MATERIALS: 4" x 5" White felt • White ½" ribbon • 2 White ribbon roses with stem • 50 seed beads (Pink, Clear) • *DMC* White floss

White Dress
MATERIALS: 3" x 5" White felt • 1½" Pink and White Flower ribbon ½" wide • 50 seed beads (Pink, Clear) • *DMC* White floss

Wedding Cake
MATERIALS: 3" x 5" White felt • Flowers with Leaves (6 White, 6 Pink) • *DMC* Pink floss

Wedding Mini-Clothing Patterns

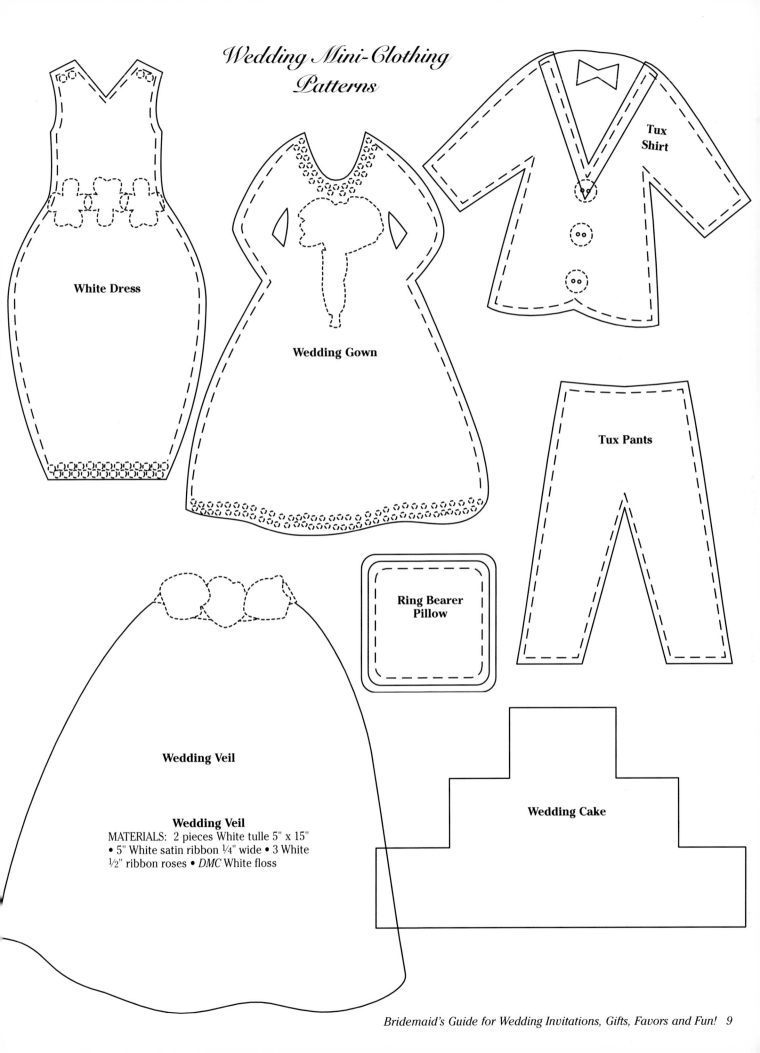

White Dress

Wedding Gown

Tux Shirt

Tux Pants

Ring Bearer Pillow

Wedding Veil

Wedding Veil
MATERIALS: 2 pieces White tulle 5" x 15"
• 5" White satin ribbon ¼" wide • 3 White
½" ribbon roses • *DMC* White floss

Wedding Cake

BASIC MATERIALS:
14 new bills • 1½ yards of ribbon • 2-Way glue • Drinking straw • Tape
INSTRUCTIONS:
Make 2 hearts, 2 butterflies, 3 rosettes and 2 half rosettes. • Tape a 1" piece of drinking straw to the backs of the hearts. • String all pieces together. Tie ribbon ends together.

Folded Rosette

MATERIALS:
1 new bill for half rosette and 2 new bills for rosette • Silk flower with wire stem • 2-Way glue

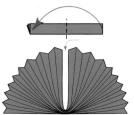

1. For half rosette, accordion fold bill 8 times. Or fan fold 16 times.

2. Fold bill in half. Glue edges together.

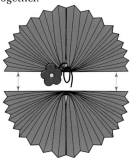

3. Open into fan shape. Wrap wire stem of flower through fold to secure.

4. For rosette, make 2 half rosettes. Attach a flower to one rosette. Glue 2 half rosette edges together.

Money Necklace for Good Luck and Good Fortune

by Norma Eng

Make this dollar bill money necklace for a wedding shower, or 'bride's night out' gift.

It is traditional to pin money to the bride and groom (during a dance) at the reception. Giving dollars always creates excitement and sends best wishes to the new couple for heartfelt happiness.

Folded Heart

MATERIALS: 1 new dollar bill
INSTRUCTIONS: Make heart. Insert message in front fold of heart.

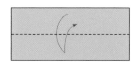
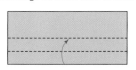

1. Fold a bill in half and crease.

2. Fold the bottom edge to the center crease.

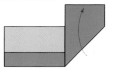

3. Fold the right side to match left side. Open fold.

4. Fold the bottom to the center crease.

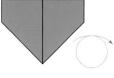
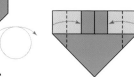

5. Repeat on the other side. Turn over.

6. Fold right and left edges to meet other fold.

7. Fold top edges down to the center.

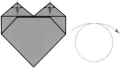

8. Fold top corners down like this.

9. Fold the top points down. Turn the bill over for heart.

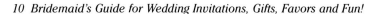

Folded Butterfly

MATERIALS:
2 new bills • 24 gauge Purple wire • Beads (18mm x 30mm Purple teardrop, 9mm Pink disk, 9mm Yellow faceted) • Wire cutters • Round-nose pliers

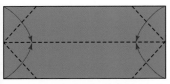

1. Fold one bill in half. Unfold. Fold corners to center crease.

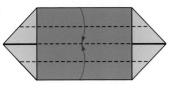

2. Fold top and bottom edges to center crease.

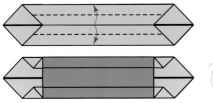

3. Fold top and bottom edges to back. Paper will look like this.

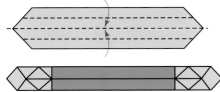

4. Turn over, bring top and bottom edges to center. Paper will look like this.

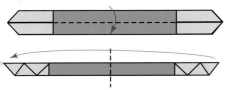

5. Fold in half. Mountain fold in half.

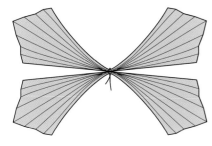

6. Open bill to resemble fan. Repeat for 2nd bill. Attach at center with 6" of wire. Do not cut off excess wire.

7. Cut two 12" pieces of Purple wire. Spiral 2" on one end of wires. Insert ends in teardrop, disk and faceted beads. Twist together above faceted bead to secure. Curl remaining wire around pencil for antennae. Using excess wire, attach body to butterfly below faceted bead. Wrap wire to back and cut off excess.

Bachelorette Parties

Bachelorette parties have been a wedding tradition for a long time.

Who Hosts?

Virtually anyone can host a party. Often the maid of honor and bridesmaids, who are close to the bride, do the honors, but any friend, relative (a cousin, for example), or even coworkers who feel the urge can plan this party.

The Guest List

Chances are that most bachelorette party guests -- who are generally the bride's best gal pals -- are wedding guests, too, but it's fine to invite coworkers or neighbors who may not be invited to a small or out-of-town wedding. Just be up front with them about your limited wedding guest list -- you don't want to disappoint any well-wishers. It's usually best to keep this party pretty small -- definitely fewer than 20 and fewer than 10 is probably ideal.

Decide on a Date

Steer clear of the night before the wedding. The rehearsal dinner is usually scheduled for that night. If the wedding is in a town other than the bride's hometown, you might want to have the party before she leaves; even if the wedding is local, party at least 2 or 3 nights before the big day.

Plan Ahead

One person can plan the entire bash, or several people (like the bridesmaids or the clique from college) can collaborate. Some bachelorette hosts ask for a donation from each guest or co-host, depending on the type of party -- whether you're renting a private room in a restaurant or taking everyone for an afternoon of spa treatments, for example. That contribution may range from $50 to $200, but the bride should not have to contribute a dime. Be reasonable and don't go overboard -- you needn't put yourself in debt over this. A fabulous time can be had by all for little money.

Spread the Word

Store-bought invitations will do, or make your own with words from your computer plus paper, scissors, pens, and glue. Choose or design with a theme in mind, even if it's as simple as the bride's favorite color. Some hostesses forego official invitations and just call guests a few weeks before the wedding -- it all depends on the type of party you're planning. If you need to make reservations for a show or other activity, you'll probably want guests to officially RSVP. If you'll be hanging out at the corner dinner dive, scrap the invites -- a phone call is probably fine. The important thing is for all to have fun!

Party Time

Bachelorette parties are more laid-back and less structured than traditional bridal showers. You can paint the town red if that's your style. But there are lots of other ways to celebrate -- a nice dinner at someone's house or a favorite restaurant, dancing at a club, the list is endless. Just make sure to have a good time. Let the bride let her hair down.

Handmade Paper Dress

Encase your invitations in colorful envelopes that are quick and easy to make.

Basic Paper Casting

MATERIALS:
Plain (no pattern) facial tissue • Rubber stamp with a wedding image or words • Towel • Radiant Pearls paint • Scissors • Spray fixative

INSTRUCTIONS:
1. Layer 10 squares of facial tissues.
2. Run under water to soak tissue. Wring as much water as you can out of the tissues.
3. Turn stamp rubber side up and place wet tissues on the stamp.
4. With a dry towel, press out as much water as possible. Rotate towel to keep it dry.
5. For a torn edge look, slowly pull excess tissue away from stamp using the wood edge of the stamp for a guide.
6. Carefully lift tissue off the stamp and lay it aside to dry for 24 hours.
7. Trim paper edges with scissors. Paint image with Radiant Pearls. Spray with fixative.

Dress Card

MATERIALS:
7" x 10" Lime Green cardstock • 4$\frac{1}{2}$" x 6$\frac{1}{2}$" Yellow flower print paper • *Inkadinkado* dress rubber stamp • 4 flower photo corners • Glue

INSTRUCTIONS:
1. Make the paper cast dress.
2. Print, write or stamp invitation on cardstock.
3. Fold cardstock in the center and crease well.
4. Glue dress on the center of the card.
5. Place photo corners on card.

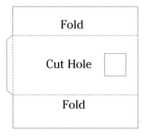

Sleeve Diagram

Basic Sleeve & Card

MATERIALS:
Cardstock or Vellum • Ribbon • 1$\frac{1}{4}$" Circle punch, $\frac{1}{8}$" Circle punch • Optional: 1$\frac{5}{8}$" Square punch or craft knife • Decorative edge scissors • Glue

INSTRUCTIONS:
Sleeve:
1. Trace or copy the pattern. Cut out cardstock or vellum on solid lines, score on dotted lines. Fold and crease well.
2. Fold sides together and glue in place. Fold up bottom flap and glue in place.
3. Punch a half circle in the open end of the card. Optional: Punch a square close to the open end.
Card:
1. Cut and/or layer 5$\frac{1}{4}$" cardstock to fit inside the sleeve.
2. Print, stamp or write invitation on cardstock.
3. Punch a hole at the top of cardstock.
4. Thread ribbon through the hole and tie a knot. Trim the ends of ribbon.

Sleeve Pattern

Pull-Out Invitations

Create wonderfully fun pull-out invitations. Pretty paper sleeves hold the cards. Pull the bow up to reveal the message inside the sleeve.

Use them as invitations for a bridal shower, wedding or those very important thank you notes.

1. Cut out the sleeve, fold and crease well.

2. Punch a half circle in the end of sleeve to make room for the ribbon.

3. Glue sleeve seam. Fold up the bottom and glue.

4. Punch one or two holes in the top of the card, thread ribbon through holes and tie a knot.

Yellow Shower

6¹/₈" x 11¹/₂" Yellow cardstock
• 5¹/₈" square Blue cardstock
• 4⁷/₈" square White cardstock
• 12" Yellow 2" wide ribbon
INSTRUCTIONS:
1. Follow instructions for sleeve and card.
2. Glue the printed White invitation to Blue cardstock.
3. Slide into sleeve.

Pink Wedding

6¹/₈" x 11¹/₂" Pink cardstock
• 5" square White cardstock
• 12" Pink 2" wide sheer ribbon • Photo
INSTRUCTIONS:
1. Follow instructions for sleeve and card.
2. Slide into sleeve.

Vellum Flower

MATERIALS: 6¹/₈" x 11¹/₂" flower vellum • 5¹/₈" square Purple cardstock • 4⁷/₈" square White cardstock • 12" of Lavender 2" wide ribbon
INSTRUCTIONS:
1. Follow instructions for sleeve and card.
2. Glue the printed White invitation to Purple cardstock.
3. Slide into sleeve.

Wedding Invitations

Ideally, guests should receive their invitation six weeks before the wedding. Since the invitation gives your guests their first impression of your wedding, you want the invitation to reflect the tone of the day. Think of your invitation as a sneak preview. Use colors and styles that will be seen at the wedding.

Don't forget to include a self-addressed, stamped RSVP card that includes a date for its return.

1. Trace the pattern, cut out and score on the dotted lines.

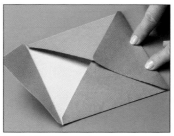

2. Fold the envelope and crease well.

3. Place the invitation inside the envelope.

4. Fold envelope together and tie with a ribbon or seal.

Maid of Honor

The maid of honor has the most responsibilities. She should also remember that listening to the bride, making her laugh, and offering emotional support is part of the honor. Here is a list of what to expect:

☐ *Lead the bridesmaids. Make sure all bridesmaids get their dresses, go to dress fittings, and find the right jewelry.*

☐ *Help shop for dresses.*

☐ *Spread the news about where the bride and groom are registered.*

☐ *Host a shower for the bride.*

☐ *Attend all pre-wedding parties.*

☐ *Keep a record of all the gifts received at various parties and showers.*

☐ *Plan the bachelorette party with the bridesmaids.*

☐ *See to it that all bridesmaids get to the rehearsal.*

☐ *Make sure that all bridesmaids get their hair and makeup done, get to the ceremony on time, and have the correct bouquets.*

☐ *Hold the groom's ring during the ceremony. The thumb is the safest place.*

☐ *Arrange the bride's train and veil before the ceremony begins and just after she arrives at the altar.*

☐ *You also might need to help the bride with her dress for the reception. Take off the train or button the bustle up to the back of the dress.*

Envelope Pattern

4-Fold Envelope Invitations

Encase your invitations in colorful envelopes that are quick and easy to make.

Basic Envelope
MATERIALS:
Patterned paper, Cardstock or Vellum • Ribbon • Glue stick
INSTRUCTIONS:
1. Trace or copy the pattern.
2. Cut on solid lines, score on dotted lines. Fold well.
3. Place an invitation inside.
4. Fold and seal or tie with a ribbon.

Mauve Envelope
MATERIALS: 8" square of Mauve cardstock • 4" square of Ivory cardstock • 18" of Mauve 3" wide sheer ribbon • Glue stick
INSTRUCTIONS:
1. Make envelope with Mauve cardstock.
2. Print or write shower information on the 4" square of Ivory.
3. Center invitation inside the envelope.
4. Fold envelope, wrap with ribbon and tie a bow.

Blue Wedding Invitation
MATERIALS: 8" square of Light Blue cardstock • 5" square of Blue cardstock • 4$3/4$" square of Ivory cardstock • 12"of $1/2$" wide Blue sheer ribbon • 36" of White $1 1/2$" wide sheer ribbon • $1/4$" Hole punch
INSTRUCTIONS:
1. Make envelope with Light Blue cardstock.
2. Print or write wedding information on the Ivory cardstock.
3. Center Ivory on Blue cardstock.
4. Punch two $1/4$" holes at the top of invitation.
5. Pull ends of Blue $1/2$" ribbon through the holes and tie a bow.
6. Center invitation inside the envelope.
7. Fold envelope, wrap with ribbon and tie a bow.

Floral Wedding Invitation
MATERIALS: 8" square of Grey-Green cardstock • 5" square of Floral cardstock • 4$3/4$" square of Vellum • 36" of Cream $1 1/2$" wide sheer ribbon • Glue stick
INSTRUCTIONS:
1. Make envelope with Grey-Green cardstock.
2. Print or write wedding information on a 4" square of vellum.
3. Center vellum on floral cardstock. Tack corners with glue.
4. Center invitation inside the envelope.
5. Fold envelope, wrap with ribbon and tie a bow.

Cut Slits for Ribbon

Poly Shrink Invitations

It's easy to add any design you desire when you shrink a stamped and colored art image.

MATERIALS:

8½" x 11" Red textured cardstock • White cardstock: 3½" x 5" & 4" x 8½" • *Ducks in a Row* bride and groom rubber stamp • Black permanent pigment ink • 16" of Red ⅞" sheer ribbon • Permanent markers (Red, Black) • Glue stick • E6000 adhesive

INSTRUCTIONS:

1. Make a poly shrink bride and groom.
2. Score and fold one end of Red cardstock in 2". Score and fold in half.
3. Make a small cut in the center of the 2" fold.
4. Slide a ribbon through the opening, Glue 2" flap to form a pocket.
5. Write invitation and reception information on White cardstock.
6. Glue invitation to the inside of front, making sure that the ribbon continues under the invitation. Insert reception card in 2" pocket.
7. Fold the card in half and tie, trim the ribbon ends.
8. Glue bride and groom on the front of card.

1. Sand poly shrink up and down, and then sand from side to side.

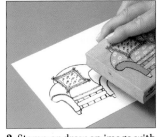

2. Stamp or draw an image with permanent pigment ink or pen.

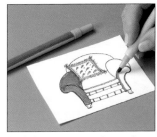

3. Color image with markers. Shrink (follow instructions on package).

Spinner Invitations

An interactive card allows you to spin a wheel to reveal the hidden message. It is fun to see different bits of information, fortunes, words and images in the square window.

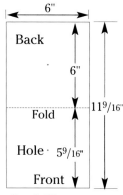

6"

Back	
	6"
Fold	
Hole · 5⁹/₁₆"	11⁹/₁₆"
Front	

Card Diagram

Basic Spinner

MATERIALS:
6" x 12" cardstock • 2 colors of cardstock for spinner • Paper brad • 1⁵/₈" Square punch or craft knife • Glue

INSTRUCTIONS FOR CIRCLE SPINNER:
1. Trace or copy circles. Cut out 2 circles.
2. Make a tiny hole through the center of the circles.
3. Glue circles together.

FOR THE CARD:
1. Trace or draw the card shape (follow diagram). Cut out card.
2. Make a tiny hole in the center of card back (follow diagram).
3. Score the card. Fold and crease the card well.
4. Punch or cut a square at the center top of the front panel.
5. Place the circle in the card and mark areas for adding information. Remove, write information and add any stickers to the circle. You should be able to use 3 or 4 pieces of information.
6. Place the circle in the center of the folded card. Punch a brad through the holes and flatten the ends on the back of the card.
7. Glue the sides of the card together leaving the circle free to turn.

Lavender - Invitation

MATERIALS:
Cardstock (Lavender, Ivory)
INSTRUCTIONS:
1. Follow instructions and make a square spinner card.

Ivory - Bridal Shower Card

MATERIALS:
Cardstock (Green, White, Periwinkle, Peach) • Optional: Decorative scissors
INSTRUCTIONS:
1. Follow instructions and make a square spinner card.
Optional: Trim the top of front fold with decorative scissors.
2. Cut 5¹/₄" square of Peach cardstock and place inside card.

Grey - Round the Clock Shower Card

MATERIALS:
Cardstock (Metallic Dark Grey, Metallic White) • 1 Clock button • 8" White 3" wide sheer ribbon • E6000 adhesive
INSTRUCTIONS:
1. Follow instructions and make a square spinner card.
2. Thread ribbon through the back of the clock button. Adhere button on the center of the paper brad. Trim ends of ribbon.

1. Make a tiny hole in the center of the card and circle.

2. Punch a square or circle in the top of the card.

3. Insert brad through holes in the card and circle.

4. Glue the sides of the card together. Do not glue circle.

Basic Basket Card

MATERIALS:
Cardstock for basket • Cardstock for card • Scrap of cardstock for the 'spring' • Acrylic spray sealer • Craft knife • Glue stick

INSTRUCTIONS FOR FRONT:
1. Trace or copy basket pattern on cardstock.
2. Cut out the basket.
3. Use a craft knife to cut out the center of the basket handle (on the front only).
4. Decorate card as desired.
5. To make a paper 'spring' that allows the card to stand open, cut a piece of cardstock ½" x 1¾".
6. Fold the 'spring' in half. Fold each end up to the center fold.
7. Glue one end to the front of basket and glue the other end to the top back of basket. Let dry.
8. Add a ribbon bow to the basket handle.

FOR CARD:
9. Cut cardstock to 3" x 6". Fold in half to make a 3" square card.
10. Write or stamp a message on the inside.
11. Glue on back of card covering ribbon ends and making a prop for the card.

Ivory Wedding Basket

MATERIALS: Ivory embossed cardstock • Ivory cardstock • 24" each of ⅝" ribbon (Ivory, Moss Green) • Small Pink ribbon rose • Green pigment ink • Metallic Gold paint pen • Tacky glue • Glue stick

INSTRUCTIONS:
Cut basket and handle from Ivory embossed cardstock . • Cut basket without handle from cardstock. • Edge with Gold paint pen. Wrap handle snugly with Green ribbon using glue to hold ends in place. Wrap loosely with Ivory ribbon, glue the ends to secure. Twist a length of Green ribbon and wrap it across basket. Glue ends flat on back. Tie a bow. Glue bow and rose on handle.

Green Standing Basket Card

MATERIALS: Green cardstock • Ivory cardstock • Metallic Gold floral stickers • Green pigment ink • Rainbow inkpad • Metallic Gold paint pen • Chalk (Pink, Green, Yellow) • 24" of Mauve ⅝" wide ribbon • Small round sponge • Acrylic spray sealer • Glue stick

INSTRUCTIONS:
Cut basket and handle from Green cardstock. • Cut basket without handle from cardstock. • Sponge rainbow ink around edges of Ivory basket. • Place stickers on Ivory card. Color with chalk. Spray with sealer. • Trim basket with Gold paint pen. • Add ribbon bow to basket handle.

Pretty Basket Invitations

Little baskets are a terrific way to show how much you care. Create unusual invitations with their own personality.

Send a basket full of cheerful greetings. Each basket blooms with color, charm and natural beauty.

Fold

Glue a folded card prop to the back of basket.

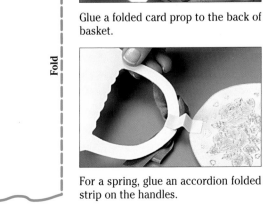

For a spring, glue an accordion folded strip on the handles.

Timeless Love

When you need a soft, subtle background pattern on your canvas, consider this faux technique. It is very simple to do and the results can be breathtaking.

continued from page 3
MATERIALS:
Three 8" x 8" canvases • 4 hinges • Acrylic paint (Sage, Parchment) • Faux Paint Medium • Van Dyke Brown ink • Pattern paper • Clock Kit • Ribbon • Key & Lock Charms • Letter stickers • Wood circle to fit clock • Chipboard • Large artist sponge • Drill • Sewing machine • Thread • Photo tape • Tacky glue

INSTRUCTIONS:
1. Apply a mixture of equal parts Sage paint and Faux paint medium to all 3 canvases with a large sponge. • Ink the edges of all canvases. • Hinge canvases together 1" from the top and bottom. • Cut patterned papers and chipboard: Two 6" x 7½", one 6" square. • Sew a zigzag stitch around each paper.
2. Adhere chipboard to the back of each paper, ink the edges. • Apply photo and letter stickers to each 6" x 7½" piece. • Adhere patterned paper backed with chipboard to the canvases. • Paint the wood circle with Parchment.
• Drill a hole in the middle of the wood circle. • Ink edges of the wood circle.
3. Cut a piece of pattern paper to fit the center of wood circle. • Ink the edges of paper. • Adhere paper to wood. • Punch a small hole in the middle of center canvas. • Tie ribbons and charms around the edge of the two outer canvases. • Adhere the wood circle to the middle of the center canvas. • Adhere the face of the clock to the wood circle. • Add clock mechanism and hands following the manufacturer's instructions.

1. Sponge paint mixture onto canvases.

2. Mark the holes for the hinges.

3. Adhere sewn paper to chipboard.

4. Ink the edges of the paper/chipboard.

5. Cut a hole in the center of the canvas.

6. Adhere the clock face to the wood.

7. Assemble the clockworks from the back of the canvas.

8. Assemble the clock hands from the front.

Wrapped 3-Panel Card

It is very simple to create a wrapping.

MATERIALS:
Lilac mulberry paper with Silver threads • 5" x 15" Black cardstock • 2 yards Silver metallic thread • Brass heart charm • Tape • Glue stick

INSTRUCTIONS:
1. Fold Black cardstock into three 5" sections.
2. Cut mulberry paper 5½" x 11".
3. Wrap short end of mulberry paper around ruler and continue wrapping until all paper is loosely on ruler.
4. Push wrapped paper down to bottom creating tiny folds and pleats. Remove carefully and unroll but do not stretch out wrinkles. Open card. Place pleated mulberry paper across center panel and wrap ends around the back about 1½" on each side. Tape ends on back of card.
5. Gather pleated mulberry in center with Silver thread folded over and over to about 7".
6. Tie thread in double knot around handmade paper making sure knot is in center.
7. Cover back of first panel with glue and press in place behind decorated panel.
8. Loosely tie charm around center of pleated paper.

1. Wrap mulberry paper around ruler, pleat.

2. Glue ends of pleated paper inside card.

3. Tie charm in center of pleated paper.

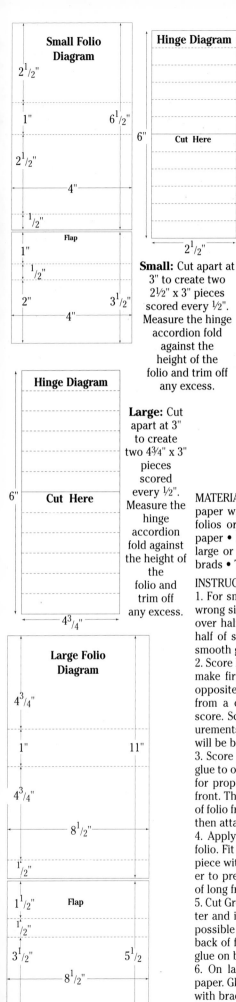

Small Folio Diagram

2 1/2"
1"   6 1/2"
6"
2 1/2"
4"
1/2"
Flap
1"
1/2"
2"   3 1/2"
4"

Hinge Diagram

Cut Here

2 1/2"

Small: Cut apart at 3" to create two 2½" x 3" pieces scored every ½". Measure the hinge accordion fold against the height of the folio and trim off any excess.

Hinge Diagram

6"   **Cut Here**

4 3/4"

Large: Cut apart at 3" to create two 4¾" x 3" pieces scored every ½". Measure the hinge accordion fold against the height of the folio and trim off any excess.

Large Folio Diagram

4 3/4"
1"   11"
4 3/4"
8 1/2"
1/2"
Flap
1 1/2"
1/2"
3 1/2"   5 1/2
8 1/2"

MATERIALS: 20" x 26" heavy textured mulberry paper with floral inclusions to make 4 to 5 small folios or one large folio • Scrap of Green heavy paper • 24" Moss Green ⅝" wide sheer ribbon for large or 18" for small folio • Cutting mat • Small brads • Tacky glue

INSTRUCTIONS:

1. For small and large folios, place paper flat with wrong side up. Squiggle generous amounts of glue over half of sheet. Spread glue evenly. Fold other half of sheet over to make a double thick sheet, smooth gently. Cut out folio pieces.

2. Score lightly on wrong side. Start at one end and make first 2 scores then rotate paper and score opposite end as indicated. It is easier to measure from a cut end than to measure from score to score. Score sides first to exactly the same measurements. The space left between the side scores will be bottom of folio.

3. Score pleated side hinges lightly. Apply bead of glue to outside pleats of hinges. Referring to photo for proper placement, glue to wrong side of folio front. The first fold of hinge should align with edge of folio front. Wait a few minutes for the glue to set, then attach hinges to back of folio. Allow to dry.

4. Apply glue to ½" flap extending from back of folio. Fit flap into ½" space scored on pattern flap piece with long part of flap in front. Use bone folder to press pieces together firmly. Round corners of long front flap if desired.

5. Cut Green paper into 1" circle. Punch hole in center and insert small brass brad, opening as far as possible to make brad lay flat. Determine center back of folio and glue ribbon down. Place drop of glue on brad assembly and glue over ribbon.

6. On large folio, cut 1½" circle from mulberry paper. Glue in place over ribbon. Glue Green paper with brad in place. Let dry.

Handmade Paper Folios

A container as treasured as the photos, thoughtful notes and memories it holds… this folio made with floral mulberry is sure to become a cherished family heirloom.

1. Glue pleated hinges to both sides of folio.

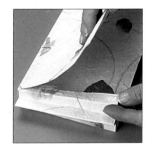

2. Join front of folio to back of folio.

3. Attach flap to back of folio.

4. Finish with ribbon closure.

Embossed metal adds a rich gleam to the front of simple cards. Just stamp or trace, emboss and cut the silver color metal to make a classy embellishment.

Basic Embossing

MATERIALS:
Cardstock • Aluminum metal • Rubber stamp or pattern • Scrap paper • Fine point stylus • Gem-Tac adhesive

INSTRUCTIONS:
1. Stamp or draw design on a piece of scrap paper.
2. Place a piece of metal on a foam mat.
3. Place image on top of metal. Tape in place.
4. Trace over design with a stylus.
5. Cut metal to size. Adhere to card.

1. Place a cut piece of metal on a rubber mat. Tape the image on the metal. Trace the image with a fine point stylus.

2. For a debossed look, turn the metal over and retrace the image. Emboss puffy areas with a pencil eraser.

Bride & Groom

MATERIALS:
Cardstock (6" x 9" Blue, 2½" x 4¼" Peach, 3" x 4¾" Light Green) • 4" x 9" Yellow print paper • 3" x 5" of metal • *Artee Stamps* rubber stamp or a pattern • Deckle scissors
INSTRUCTIONS:
1. Follow directions for embossing metal.
2. Trim metal to 2¼" x 4".
3. Score Blue cardstock 4" from left side. Trim to 5½" x 9" with deckle scissors.
4. Fold cardstock well on the scores.
5. Print or write wedding invitation in the center of the 4" section.
6. Glue print paper inside the front flap.
7. Layer metal, Peach and Green cardstock. Glue to the center front of card.

Diamond Ring

MATERIALS:
6" x 12" Silver cardstock • 2½" x 3½" Metal • *Personal Stamp Exchange* ring rubber stamp or a pattern
INSTRUCTIONS:
1. Emboss metal.
2. Trim metal to 1½" x 2½". Fold cardstock to make a 6" square card.
3. Print or write info inside card.
4. Glue metal piece to front of card.

Framed Flowers Invitation

Shimmering ribbon inside a frame allude to a special day to come. What bride would want ordinary invitations when something this lovely is so easy to make?

MATERIALS:
6" x 8" blank card • 5" x 7" pre-cut matboard frame • Cardstock (8½" x 11" Ivory, 3" x 7¾" Lavender, 3¼" x 5¼" Lilac) • 3" x 4" White handmade paper • Pearl White paint • Small artificial flowers • 18" of Lavender 1½" wide sheer ribbon • *Inkadinkado* "words" rubber stamp • Lavender inkpad • 1/8" hole punch • Decorative scissors • Stipple brush • Light Green floral tape • Tacky glue • Glue stick

INSTRUCTIONS:
1. Paint matboard with Pearl White. Let dry.
2. Stipple front edges of card with Lavender ink.
3. Make a small bundle of flowers. Secure stems together with floral tape. Curl end of stem.
4. Cut 8" of ribbon. Tie ribbon around stem with loose knot. Place ribbon behind flowers and behind stem.
5. Glue flower bundle to Lilac cardstock. Adhere frame over flowers.
6. Stamp "words" on White paper. Trim edges with decorative scissors to 2" x 3". Glue in place.
7. Print invitation on Ivory cardstock. Cut to 5¼" x 7¾". Glue inside card. Tear Lavender cardstock to 1½" x 7¾". Adhere a strip to each side of invitation.
8. Punch 2 holes, 1" apart, at top of invitation. Insert end of ribbon into each hole. Cross ribbon on the back of invitation. Bring ribbon ends through opposite holes. Trim ribbon ends.

Center - Fold line

Arched Door Invitation

Irresistible texture on this gorgeous embossed paper entices you to run your hand across it. Pearls and the essential "something blue" elegantly invite you to open this card.

MATERIALS:
12" x 12" embossed Ivory cardstock • Blue cardstock (8½" x 11, 2½" square) • 5½" x 11" Ivory cardstock • Parchment paper • *Angelina* fusible White fibers • 3" square of cotton quilt batting • 16" ruffle ribbon • 8" pearls-by-the-yard • Iridescent glitter glue • Blue chalk • Iron • 1¾" Circle punch • 1/4" wide red liner tape • Tacky glue • Glue stick

INSTRUCTIONS:
1. Trace or copy pattern on embossed paper.
2. Cut out. Score the fold lines. Fold flaps toward the center.
3. Cut Ivory cardstock to fit the middle of card. Glue in place.
4. Make a fiber circle for inside top of card. Adhere in place.
5. Punch a 1¾" circle of embossed cardstock. Rub embossed area with Blue chalk or ink. Adhere in arch, on top of fibers.
6. Print invitation on Blue cardstock. Cut to 5" x 7".
7. Tape ribbon to back of invitation along the top edge. Adhere invitation to inside center section.
8. **Heart Accent**: Front of card is not pictured: Cut a 2¼" heart from batting. Glue batting to center of Blue 2½" square.
9. Run a bead of glitter glue around heart. Add pearls, press, dry.
10. Place parchment paper on ironing board. Pull fibers apart. Make a 4" circle of loosely piled fibers. Place another parchment paper on top. Press with an iron until fibers are fused.
11. Peel fibers off paper. Cut in half. Glue half to each front flap.
12. Glue heart embellishment card to center of left flap.
13. Apply red liner tape to edge of ruffled ribbon trim. Adhere ruffled ribbon inside the edge of the left flap.

Be the Best Bridesmaid

☐ *Help the bride choose the bridesmaid dresses... search for good deals.*

☐ *Plan a shower! Invitations must be mailed 3 weeks before the party. Talk to the bride about coed or just the girls. Also, if there are too many people for one party, consider hosting two. All bridesmaids must attend all showers.*

☐ *Keep a record of all gifts. Offer to help with thank you letters.*

☐ *Bridesmaids attend showers, the rehearsal dinner, ceremony and reception.*

☐ *Have snacks for the bride while she is getting ready.*

☐ *Bridesmaids act as hostesses at all events. Help the guests know where to sit and what to do. Keep those duties away from the bride. The bride can become overwhelmed with guests.*

☐ *Get the Party Started! When the music starts at the reception, bridesmaids are first on the floor. Set the tone for the guests.*

☐ *Try not to get frustrated when situations become stressful. Keep the bride calm.*

MATERIALS:
11" x 18" handmade paper • Ivory cardstock (5" x 8", 8½" x 11") • 8½" x 11" vellum • 1½" x 8" Aloe pearl paper • White shrink plastic • Rubber stamps (*Inkadinkado* "Love, Honor, Cherish"; *Hero Arts* Heart) • *Palette* Landscape stamp pad • *Tsukineko* inkpads (Aloe Vera VersaMagic; Peacock Brilliance) • 5" White ribbed 1" wide grosgrain ribbon • 4" Green striped 3/8" wide ribbon • 11" x 18" acetate for pattern • Permanent marker • Fine grit sandpaper • Toaster oven • Decorative scissors • Vellum tape • Tacky glue • Glue stick

INSTRUCTIONS:
1. Use permanent marker to trace folder pattern onto acetate sheet. Place pattern on handmade paper, trace pattern, cut out. Fold.
2. Use Peacock ink to stamp hearts on front edge. Trim away paper edge even with the points on the hearts.
3. Adhere Aloe pearl paper to the back of the left side, even with the edge of the hearts.
4. Crease folder on fold lines. Glue tabs on pocket edges to form pocket on right side page.
5. Make 2 shrink plastic embellishments: Lightly sand shrink plastic on both sides. Lightly color shrink plastic with Aloe Vera inkpad. Stamp "Love, Honor, Cherish" twice with Landscape inkpad. Cut 2 rectangles using decorative scissors. Shrink in toaster oven according to manufacturer's instructions.
6. Adhere shrink plastic embellishment to center front of invitation.
7. Glue 5" x 8" Ivory cardstock to inside center of folder.
8. Print invitation wording on vellum. Cut to 4" x 7". Adhere top of vellum to Ivory cardstock.
9. Adhere ribbons across top of invitation. Adhere shrink plastic embellishment to top center of ribbon.
Reception card: Print wording on Ivory cardstock. Cut to 4" x 6". Cut handmade paper 2" x 4". Fold to 1" x 4". Adhere to top of reception card.
Response card: Print wording on Ivory cardstock. Cut to 3½" x 5¼". Cut handmade paper 2" x 3½". Fold to 1" x 3½". Adhere to left side.
10. Insert reception card, response card, and envelope into pocket.

Embossed Ribbon

Professional looking invitations announce a wedding in memorable style.

MATERIALS:
7" x 8½" Aqua cardstock • 6½" x 8" Light Blue pearl paper • White pattern paper • 3" x 6½" Vellum • 6½" Light Blue 1½" wide velvet ribbon • *My Sentiments Exactly* LOVE rubber stamp • Iron • Misting bottle with water • 1/4" wide Red liner tape • Glue stick

INSTRUCTIONS:
1. Print invitation on White paper. Cut to 5½" x 6". • 2. Tear long edges of Vellum to 2½" wide. • 3. Adhere pearl paper to cardstock. Adhere invitation off center, towards the right of pearl paper. Adhere Vellum layer over left edge of invitation.
Emboss ribbon: 4. Place rubber stamp rubber side up. Place velvet ribbon, velvet side down, on rubber stamp. Lightly mist the ribbon with water. • 5. Press with a hot iron for fifteen seconds. Adjust time as needed for your iron. • 6. Adhere ribbon to card with Red liner tape.

Heart Buckle Invitation

MATERIALS:
12" square of White embossed cardstock, 7½" square of White cardstock • 6" square of Ivory cardstock • 7/8" x 2" strip of White cardstock • Heart buckle • 18" of lace 2¾" wide ribbon • 10" of White satin 5/8" wide ribbon • Needle • Thread • Glue stick

INSTRUCTIONS:
1. Make pattern on 12" paper. On each side, measure from the left edge, marking "A" at 5½" and "B" at 6½". Repeat on all four sides. Place a ruler diagonally from mark "A" to mark "B" across a corner and draw a light pencil line. Repeat for all four corners. Cut two 3" slits in center square as indicated on pattern. • 2. Cut out small triangle between marks "A" and "B" on each side. • 3. Score and fold pencil lines on all four sides. • 4. Sew one end of ribbon to buckle. Insert ribbon through slits. • 5. Glue 7½" square to inside center. 6. Print invitation wording on 6" square.
Ribbon corner mounts for inside :
6. Follow pattern to cut 4 cardstock triangles. • 7. Place ribbon across triangle, adhering with glue. Fold ribbon toward back, adhering with glue. Trim edges. • 8. Make four corners. Adhere to the invitation inside the card. • 9. Fold flaps toward center. Draw ribbon through buckle.

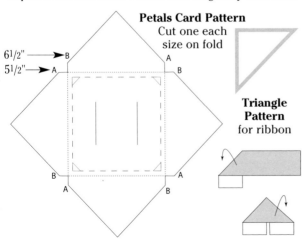

Petals Card Pattern
Cut one each
size on fold

6½" → B
5½" → A

Triangle Pattern
for ribbon

Sage Door Invitation

Your guests will enjoy receiving these unique invitations. Just open the doors to discover the details for a special celebration.

MATERIALS:
Cardstock (12" x 12" Gray, 8 1/2" x 11" Ivory) • 4" x 10" Ivory patterned paper • 4" x 8" silk dupioni fabric • 2 pearl brads • *Penny Black* stamps (Scroll background, flower) •Embossing inkpad • Silver embossing powder • 11" x 12" acetate • Permanent marker • Circle punches (1/8", 5/8", 1 1/4" 1 3/4") • Heat gun • Glue stick

INSTRUCTIONS:
1. Use marker to trace pattern onto acetate. Cut out.
2. Trace pattern on cardstock. Cut out. Score fold lines. Fold flaps towards center.
3. Stamp design across flaps with embossing ink. Apply and heat set embossing powder.
4. Cut 2 Ivory patterned papers 3 1/2" x 5".
5. Cut 2 pieces of silk, 2 1/2" x 4".
6. Glue 1 silk to center of each decorative paper. Fold silk/paper to 1 3/4" x 5".
7. Glue silk/paper to each door, matching fold to door edge.
8. Punch a 1/8" hole for each doorknob. Insert pearl brad. Open brad wings inside of card.
9. Punch two 5/8" Gray circles. Glue over brad wings inside card.
10. Punch a 1 3/4" circle from Ivory patterned paper. Punch a 1 1/4" circle from Gray paper. Stamp and emboss design on Gray circle. Glue small circle to large circle. Apply glue to 1/2 of the back of the large circle. Adhere to the left door near the peak.
11. Print invitation on Ivory cardstock. Cut to 5" x 7 1/2". Adhere inside to center back of card.

Center line

1/2" flaps

Fold line

15 3/8"

8"

3"

5 1/8"

5 1/8"

5 1/8"

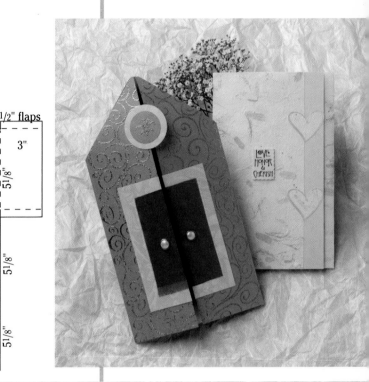

Accordion
Create programs or small albums as favors for guests.

MATERIALS:
Two 3$\frac{1}{2}$" x 5$\frac{1}{2}$" matboards • 2 pieces 3$\frac{1}{2}$" x 5$\frac{1}{2}$" cotton quilt batting • 2 pieces 4$\frac{1}{2}$" x 6$\frac{1}{2}$" White silk • Ivory pattern cardstock (5" x 18", 4" square scrap) • Ivory cardstock • 30" of sheer 1" wide ribbon • 8 flat back $\frac{1}{8}$" rhinestones • *Hero Arts* Heart rubber stamp • Black inkpad • Markers • $\frac{1}{4}$" wide red liner tape (70" per invitation) • White craft glue • Glue stick
INSTRUCTIONS:
1. Place silk on table, place batting on top, add matboard. Apply red liner tape around matboard, $\frac{1}{8}$" from edges. Fold silk towards matboard, adhering silk to tape. Working on opposite

edges, fold corners at a diagonal. Apply dabs of Tacky glue to inside corners. • 2. Score Ivory cardstock every 3", creating 6 panels. Accordion fold.
3. Cut 2 ribbons 15" long. Adhere both ribbons behind left edge of front cover. • 4. Tape first accordion section to inside cover. Repeat for last page of accordion section. • 5. Print invitation sections on decorative paper. Cut each section to 2$\frac{1}{2}$" x 4$\frac{1}{4}$". Adhere sections to accordion. • 6. Stamp 4 hearts on Ivory scrap. Color. Cut into 1$\frac{1}{2}$" squares. • 7. Adhere 2 heart squares to cover and one inside each flap. • 8. Adhere rhinestones to corners of heart squares on cover. • 9. Bring one ribbon around back of book, tie into bow at center front. Trim ribbon ends.

Sparkle Heart Invitation
A touch of vellum, the shimmer of beads and a gentle sparkling of glitter create an elegant invitation.

MATERIALS:
2 sheets 8$\frac{1}{2}$" x 11" Pearl cardstock • 8$\frac{1}{2}$" x 11" vellum paper • 8$\frac{1}{2}$" x 11" Ivory linen paper • Seed beads (White, Ivory) • Clear micro beads • *Ranger* Crystal Stickles glitter • 10" Iridescent ribbon $\frac{3}{8}$" wide • Vellum tape • 4" square Red liner sheet • Glue stick
INSTRUCTIONS:
1. Fold Pearl cardstock to 5$\frac{1}{2}$" x 8$\frac{1}{2}$".
2. Use pattern to cut 2 vellum triangles.
3. On each piece of vellum, fold back $\frac{1}{2}$" on long edge to create a flange. Apply vellum tape to flange. Align 1 flange with folded edge and the other with the open edge of invitation. Adhere flanges in place.
4. Trace pattern for hearts. Cut 1 large and 2 small hearts from red liner sheet.
5. Adhere vellum points in place with large red liner heart.
6. Mix together equal amounts of White, Ivory and Clear beads. Remove red liner from heart. Pour bead mix onto heart. Press beads with fingers to secure.
7. Draw glitter lines on diagonal edges of vellum. Let dry.
8. Print invitation on linen paper. Cut to 5" x 8". Adhere inside of card.
9. Cut 5" of ribbon. Place at center top of invitation. Secure with small red liner tape heart. Remove red liner, pour on bead mix. Press beads to secure.
Response card:
Print response card on Pearl cardstock. Cut to 3$\frac{1}{2}$" x 5". Cut 5" of ribbon, fold in half diagonally. Place on left corner of response card. Adhere with small red liner heart over ribbon. Remove liner, pour on beads. Press beads to secure.
Pocket for Response card:
Cut vellum 3" x 4$\frac{1}{2}$". Place vellum tape on 1 long and 2 short sides. Adhere inside cover, near bottom. Insert response card and return envelope into pocket.

Elegant Place Cards

MATERIALS:
Gray cardstock • 4$\frac{1}{2}$" square Ivory patterned paper • 3$\frac{1}{2}$" Ivory $\frac{1}{4}$" wide ribbon • $\frac{5}{8}$" wide paper rose • Tacky glue • Glue stick
INSTRUCTIONS:
1. Print guest names and table numbers on cardstock. Cut to measure 2" x 4".
2. Score Ivory paper and fold to 2" x 4".
3. Adhere Gray card, ribbon, and paper rose in place.

'Words of Love' Invitation
A beautiful invitation announces the special day.

MATERIALS:
6" x 18" cardstock • 6" x 9" Green pattern paper • Ivory cardstock • 3" square Tan cardstock • *One Heart One Mind* "Love" rub-on words • 6" of Beige $\frac{5}{8}$" sheer ribbon • 2 eyelets • 4 brads • 2 heart charms • 18" thin cord • Wavy scissors • Punches ($\frac{1}{8}$" & $\frac{5}{8}$" circles, 1" flower) • $\frac{1}{4}$" red liner tape • Glue stick
INSTRUCTIONS:
1. Using 6" x 18" cardstock, fold a flap 2" from one short end. • 2. Cut unfolded edge with decorative scissors. • 3. Apply red liner tape to edge of ribbon. Adhere ribbon to decorative edge. • 4. Measure 7$\frac{1}{2}$" from ribbon edge. Score and fold card. • 5. Cut Green paper 6" x 8". Punch out 6 Green flowers. • 6. Computer print invitation. Cut to 5$\frac{1}{2}$" square. Adhere to Green paper. • 7. Punch $\frac{1}{8}$" holes in four corners of invitation. • 8. Punch 6 Tan $\frac{5}{8}$" circles. Punch a $\frac{1}{8}$" hole in center of all flowers and circles. Place circle in center of flower. Insert brad to attach flowers to each corner of invitation. Adhere inside card. • 9. Punch a $\frac{1}{8}$" hole in center of folded flap, and on cover 1$\frac{3}{4}$" from center edge. Attach flower and Tan circle in each hole with an eyelet. • 10. Apply rub-ons to front cover. • 11. Fold cord in half. Insert into eyelet on flap. Insert ends through loop, draw tight. • Wrap cord around flower on cover.

FAN
Center Panel

Enlarge 400%
on a copy
machine

Cut 1

○

Fold

Fold line

**SPARKLE
HEART**
Vellum Flap
Cut 1

FAN
Side Panels

Enlarge 400%
on a copy
machine

Cut 2

○

'Words of Wisdom' Tags

*Tags can be treasured handwritten keepsakes.
Collect them and present them to the happy couple when they return from the honeymoon.*

MATERIALS: 2³/₈" x 4³/₄" Ivory tag • 9" Ivory ¹/₄" wide ribbon • ¹/₄" eyelet • Eyelet tools • Markers

INSTRUCTIONS:
1. Set eyelet in tag. • 2. Add ribbon. • 3. Place tags in a basket on the table with pens, markers, and a note asking guests to share their words of wisdom.

**FAN
Assembly
diagram**

**Fold center
panel to
the back**

○

Open Fan Invitation

*Create fan invitations that your
guests will love to receive.*

MATERIALS:
12" x 12" embossed Ivory cardstock • Two sheets 8¹/₂" x 11" Ivory cardstock • 6" x 7" clear acetate • Antique White (2¹/₄" oval label holder, ³/₈" eyelet with washer) • Small tassel • Eyelet tools • Permanent marker

INSTRUCTIONS:
1. Trace center fan section pattern onto 12" cardstock. Cut out. Fold.
2. Print "Celebrate Love" to fit inside label holder. Cut out. Attach holder to top center of fan.
3. Computer print invitation information on Ivory cardstock using a separate page for each section of the invitation. Center the text on the page.
4. Use a permanent marker to trace alignment guide onto acetate sheet. Cut out.
5. Place guide over printed page and align text with guide lines. Trace around alignment guide. Cut out section. Repeat.
6. Place invitation sections inside folded center fan section.
7. Set eyelet loosely so the fan sections will open. Add tassel.

Flower Favor Box

You may never make an ordinary bow again when vellum flowers are so easy and so unique!

Basic Folded Flower

MATERIALS:
Small gift box • Cardstock or Vellum ($5^1/2$" x $8^1/2$" for folded flower and 'ribbon', $3^1/2$" x 11" for wrapping the bow) • Gold leafing pen • 24 gauge wire • Red Liner tape

INSTRUCTIONS FOR BOX:
1. Cut a $^1/2$" x 11" strip for the 'ribbon'.
2. Wrap the box.
3. Attach the 'ribbon' wrap with tape.

FOR FOLDED FLOWER:
1. Cut three 3" squares.
2. Edge pieces with the Gold leafing pen.
3. Score and fold each square. Fold 2 squares in half.
4. Glue one folded square on each side of center square.
5. Wrap center with wire, curl the ends around a toothpick.
6. Attach flower to the top of box.

1. Cut a narrow strip of cardstock or vellum for the 'ribbon'.

2. Cut 3 squares for each flower. Optional: Color edges with a pen.

3. Score and fold each square (follow diagram).

4. Fold 2 squares in half. Glue one on each side of third square. Wrap center with wire, curl ends around a toothpick.

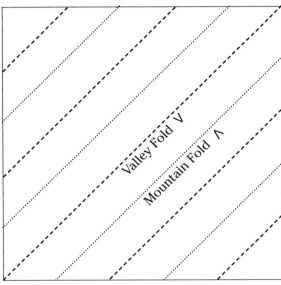

Valley Fold V

Mountain Fold ∧

Folding Template

Wedding Keepsake Card

After the wedding... help the bride thank the wedding guests with a keepsake memory card.

MATERIALS:
Papers (TeaDye, Beige) • Large White slide mount • $4^1/2$" x 6" card • Wedding cake sticker • 12" White $^1/4$" wide sheer ribbon • *Stampington* Love, Honor, Cherish rubber stamps • Inkpads (Brown, Beige) • Glue stick • E6000 adhesive

INSTRUCTIONS:
1. Cover card with TeaDye paper.
2. Stamp words in Brown ink on a $1^1/2$" square of Beige paper.
3. Sponge words lightly with both inks. Glue to card.
4. Insert a photo in the slide mount. Adhere to card.
5. Computer print names and date on cardstock. Attach to slide mount.
6. Weave sheer ribbon around the frame.
7. Adhere flowers to ribbon and slide mount with E6000.
8. Attach wedding cake sticker.

Gift and Candy Bags

These pretty containers decorate your tables and hold tasty treats.
Make little shirt bags in your wedding colors and fill them to the brim with sweet treats.

Basic Bag Instructions

MATERIALS:
8¹/2" x 11" sheet of handmade paper or cardstock • Two 2" x 3" wood rubber stamps (or a cube) • Red liner tape • Masking tape • Glue stick • Tacky glue

INSTRUCTIONS:
1. Fold a sheet of paper to 5¹/2" x 8¹/2".
2. Stack 2 stamps rubber sides together and secure with masking tape (or use a 2" x 2" cube).
3. Cut 2" x 2" cardstock to fit inside the base.
4. Place stamps on paper (2" from one short edge and ¹/2" from one long edge).
5. Pull the edges of paper snugly over the stamp gift-wrap style to make the base. Tape or glue in place.
6. Place cardstock square against base of stamps. Fold in end flaps of paper and tape or glue to cardstock square. Remove rubber stamps.

Curled Trim Bag

MATERIALS: 8¹/2" x 11" Mulberry paper (Grey and Ivory) • Skewer
INSTRUCTIONS:
1. Make bag. • 2. In corners and center of sides, make 2" to 3" long cuts down the sides of bag. • 3. Use a skewer to roll each strip down as far and as tightly as possible to curl the paper. • 4. Arrange curls as shown.

Rosebud Bag with Handle

MATERIALS: 8¹/2" x 11" Handmade paper • White cardstock • 12" Pink ⁵/8" wide sheer ribbon
INSTRUCTIONS:
1. Make bag. • To make handle, cut cardstock 1" x 8¹/2". • 2. Run a thin bead of glue down center and fold in half lengthwise. Glue ends inside the bag. • 3. Make a ribbon bow and glue to side of handle.

1. Fold paper around stacked rubber stamps or a cube shape.

2. Fold down ends, gift-wrap style and tape or glue in place.

Mini Shirt Bags

White - Tux Shirt Mini Bag

MATERIALS:
8¹/2" x 11" White mulberry paper • White cardstock • Black cardstock • 12" Black ³/8" wide ribbon • ¹/4" hole punch
INSTRUCTIONS:
1. To make collar, fold down one long edge ³/4", fold over again.
2. Placing paper with collar folds down, make bag.
3. Glue closed in front and up to collar.
4. Fold corners of collar back and glue on bow.
5. Punch Black buttons from cardstock, glue on front.
Optional: Make a liner with an 8" x 5" piece of White cardstock to create a sturdier bag. Cut a V shape in front of liner to match the collar shape.

Red - Shirt Mini Bag

MATERIALS: 8¹/2" x 11" Red mulberry paper • Red cardstock • 12" White ³/8" wide ribbon
Instructions are the same as above.

Insert a cardstock liner into the mulberry paper bag.

Scrapbook Pages

MATERIALS:
White cardstock • White vellum • Paper cut-outs • Assorted White fibers • Decorative scissors • Double-sided tape

INSTRUCTIONS:
1. Cut cardstock to frame photo and announcement.
2. Wind fibers around frame, knotting the ends together.
3. Cover scrapbook page with vellum.
4. Glue adorned frame over photo or invitation.
5. Glue fibers around edges of page. Adhere cut-outs to corners.

1. Cut out cardstock frame and wrap with fibers.

2. Glue vellum on the scrap book page.

Album

by Pattie Donham

MATERIALS:
Scrapbook covered with White handmade paper • 2 sheets White handmade paper • ½ yard sheer White fabric • White fibers • Plastic sheet • Heart applique • Basting spray • Photo • White thread • Sewing machine with Zigzag stitch • Straight pins • Hot glue

INSTRUCTIONS:
1. Place open album on fabric and cut 2" from edges on all sides. Set album aside.
2. Lightly spray fabric with basting spray. Let dry for a few minutes. Place fibers over entire fabric surface making swirls and circles as desired. Press fibers into fabric with fingers. Let dry for another 30 minutes or until tackiness disappears.
3. Zigzag stitch adorned fabric in a 1" grid pattern over entire piece to secure fibers.
4. From sheer fabric, cut photo pocket 1" larger than photo.
5. Cut plastic same size as photo.
6. Place photo in desired spot on adorned fabric. Pin plastic and sheer fabric over photo. Sew a Straight stitch on all sides.
7. Place open album on unadorned side of fabric. Fold fabric to inside cover of album and secure with glue.
8. Glue sheets of handmade paper to inside front and back of album, cover raw edges of fabric.
9. Tie a bow with fibers and glue to top left corner of photo. Glue heart above bow.
10. Glue fibers and title to first page of album.

1. Place album cover on fabric, cut around edges leaving 2" for overlap.

2. Apply the Basting Spray to the fabric. Let dry for a few minutes.

3. Press fibers on fabric in random pattern. Sew fibers in a 1" grid pattern to secure.

4. Tie fiber bow. Glue bow and heart on cover.

5. Glue fibers and title to first page of album.

Wedding Album

What a wonderful gift!

These pages are so pretty, they would look fabulous framed. The opening page is adorned with cut out letters and fibers. Your title page can be made to reflect any message you desire. One thing is for sure, when you decorate a personalized wedding album it is sure to become a cherished heirloom that will be enjoyed for years to come!

This wedding album cover is easy to make from fabric and fiber. It is sewn in a simple grid pattern. Decorated with a bow and heart... understated elegance at its best.

CAKE PATTERN

Great Shower Idea

Ask guests to bring photos of the bride to a scrapbook shower. Have a Polaroid camera ready to take pictures of the bride and guests. Supply paper and accessories. This is just as good as a game. Guests love to make something special, and the bride will cherish it forever.

Scrapbook Shower!

A great idea is a Scrapbook Shower. Invite 8 to 12 guests, have basic supplies ready, then let everyone make a page or two to go in the bride's album for after the wedding.

Of course, you'll need to leave blank 4¹⁄₂" x 6¹⁄₂" mats for the photos. All the bride will need to do is paste in the photos after the wedding... for the best wedding album ever.

A wonderful gesture is to make a gorgeous cake page for the bride's album.

Wedding Cake Page

by Christy Lemond

MATERIALS:
12" x 12" cardstock (Pink, Light Green, White) • Light Green polka dot paper • Stickers (Wedding, Pink flowers) • 4mm White pearls by the yard • Pop dots • Glue

INSTRUCTIONS:
1. Trace cake pattern on White cardstock. Tear or cut out pieces. Glue pearls and flowers in place.
2. Cut Light Green cardstock 11¹⁄₂" x 11¹⁄₂". Adhere to Pink cardstock.
3. Cut Polka Dot mats ¹⁄₂" larger than photo. Glue in place.
4. Apply wedding stickers. Adhere cake to page.

Bridal Showers: The Basics

Traditionally, a shower is a party for the bride and her closest female relatives and friends, where she is "showered" with love, good wishes and gifts.

Pick the Right Date

A shower can take place six months before the wedding or it can be the week before. It can be a surprise for the bride -- or not. Depending on where most of the guests live, you may need to schedule it far in advance so everyone can make their travel plans. If most people are local, you'll have more options. Once you've picked a date, set up a planning schedule. Talk with the bridesmaids and come up with ways to delegate duties and expenses.

The Location

You can be as creative as you want about where to have the shower. Here are some options: a picnic in a park or at the beach; a backyard barbecue; a hotel salon; a botanic garden; a tea party room. Keep in mind that party spaces get booked early in busy seasons, like during the holidays. Call about availability.

The Guest List

Everyone invited to the shower should also be invited to the wedding. Ask the bride to help out with the shower guest list. If it's a surprise, consult with her mom, groom, or sister. If it's a bridal shower (just the girls), make sure the bride's and groom's close female relatives are invited, all the women in the wedding party and the bride's close girlfriends. If it's a couples shower, make it a coed guest list.

The Gifts

It's a good idea to suggest that the bride and groom register for gifts prior to the shower. In the shower invitations, include information about where guests can purchase presents. (Yes, this is proper etiquette.)

The Invitations

Handmade invitations are more personal. Make sure guests RSVP to someone by a date that's at least a couple weeks before the shower. If many guests will be coming from out of town, mail the invitations at least two months before the party -- if not earlier -- so those who need to can make travel arrangements. If it's an in-town event, three to five weeks should be enough time.

Plan the Menu

If you're having an at-home shower, think about having the party catered. Are the bride and groom honeymooning in Venice? Do an Italian theme with a full-on pasta bar. Don't forget hors d'oeuvres. Have a fun cake made up for the shower. Wilton has fun cake toppers of the bride dragging the groom.

Memory Wire Jewelry

Quick to make and pretty to wear.

MATERIALS:
Mahogany Assortment glass beads • 54 Root Beer E beads • 18" Memory Wire necklace • 3 Gold 2" head pins • Gold ball and loop earring findings • Needle-nose pliers • Round-nose pliers • Super glue,

EARRING

Head Pin Loop
Glass Beads
E Beads
E Bead
Head Pin

TIPS: Measure your neck, allow 3" for overlap and cut wire. Hold wire with pliers where you want to cut and bend back and forth until it breaks. Do not use wire cutters as the wire is very hard and will damage your tool.

1. Pour out beads, sort large ones. Pick out 2 sets of 3 matching beads for head pins. Use 3 large beads for the center.

2. For earrings, thread 2 head pins as shown. Bend pin at right angle, trim to $3/8$" and make a loop. Attach to earrings.

3. For necklace, make dangle. Then alternate E beads with large beads until you have filled both sides of wire leaving about $3/8$" on each end.

4. Use round-nose pliers to make loops.

Center Bead

Loop

Make a loop at the end of wire and thread beads to center bead.

Make loop in head pin.

Glass Beads

E Bead

NECKLACE

Head Pin

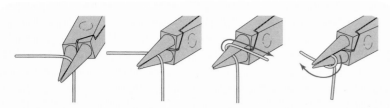

To Make Pearl Lnks:
Cut a 4" long piece of 22 gauge wire. Grasp the wire with round-nose pliers about 1¼" from the top. Bend the wire at a 90° angle. • Loosen your grip on the pliers and pivot them from horizontal to vertical. • Wrap the short piece of wire over the top jaw of the pliers as shown. • Reposition the wire on the bottom jaw of the pliers. • Complete the loop by wrapping the short end of the wire around the bottom jaw of the pliers. • Remove the loop and hold it in place as shown.

Dangles Necklace

Hang elegant pearls and crystals from a casual white or blue suede band...how simple!

MATERIALS:
7 Swarovski 10mm pearls
3 Swarovski 6mm cubes
2 Swarovski 5mm nail heads
3 Swarovski 4mm bicones
2 Swarovski 4mm rounds
24" of 22 gauge Sterling wire
5 twisted 6mm jump rings
11 Sterling 1½" ball head pins
Round-nose pliers
CORD FOR NECKLACE:
40" of Ivory rattail or Blue suede cord

Wrap the wire around the top jaw of your pliers as shown.

Move the piece to the bottom jaw of the pliers and complete the loop.

Without touching the pearl, begin coiling the shorter piece of wire around the longer piece. Begin your coils as close to the loop as possible. Make two or three coils then clip the end of wire close to the coils.

Repeat to make 5 more pearl links.

Without touching the long end of the wire, begin coiling the shorter piece of wire around the longer piece. Begin the coils as close to the loop as possible. Make two or three coils, then clip the end of wire close to the coils.

Thread on one of the pearls. Grasp the wire with pliers about ⅛" from the end of the jaws. Bend the wire at a 90° angle. Pivot your pliers from horizontal to vertical.

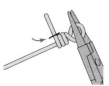

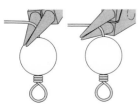

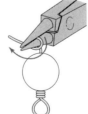

To make the dangles:
Thread each of the crystals and the last pearl on head pins and make wrapped loops with each one by following the instructions for the second half of the pearl links.

Use twisted jump rings to connect the pearl links and to hold the dangles in place. To open a jump ring, twist it to the side as shown.

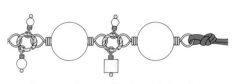

Connect the pearl links and dangles according to the pattern above.
Cut the cord in half.
Thread one piece of cord through the last pearl link on each side.
Center the link on the cord and tie an overhand knot as shown below.

To make the loop closure:
Tie two overhand knots 1" apart at the end of one side of necklace cord (hold both pieces together when tying knots). Clip ends close to the last knot.

To make the pearl toggle:
Thread loose ends of remaining piece of cord through the loop of the pearl dangle and tie an overhand knot.

Dot knot with glue before trimming close.

Pearl Goddess

Pearls accentuate a woman's natural beauty. These delicate gold strands show off small clusters of pearls that shimmer.

by Jane Merchant

MATERIALS:
two ½" Gold color pewter goddesses
pearls: two 10mm disks, four 6mm x 8mm
two 6mm Gold stardust beads
two Gold 6mm bead caps
pieces of Gold filled chain with
   3mm x 4mm links:
    two 1½", two 1", two ½"
eight 2" Gold filled head pins with ball ends
Gold filled figure 8 ring
two 5mm Gold filled split rings
pair of Gold filled ear wires
round-nose pliers

Thread a bead cap and a coin pearl on a head pin. Grasp the pin with pliers about ⅛" from the end of the jaws.

The pliers should be touching the top of the coin pearl. Bend wire at a 90° angle.

Pivot pliers from horizontal to vertical.

Wrap wire around the top jaw of pliers.
Reposition wire on the bottom jaw of pliers. Wrap wire around bottom jaw of pliers.

Slip straight end of head pin through the bottom link of the 1" chain and grasp the loop of the dangle with the pliers.

Without touching the pearl, begin coiling the short end around the neck of the dangle. Begin coils as close to the loop as possible.

Make 2 or 3 coils, then clip the end of the wire close to the coils.

Make dangles with remaining pearls and stardust beads and attach them to the 1" chain.

Use a split ring to connect the goddess charm to the bottom loop of the longest chain.

Thread a 1½", 1" and ½" chain on the large end of a figure 8 ring. Open ear wire loop and thread on the small end of the figure 8 ring. Close the ear wire loop.

Repeat above steps for the remaining earring.

Simple Necklace

This simple necklace will complement your silk blouse, favorite dress or a pretty T-shirt. Make it this afternoon, wear it tonight!

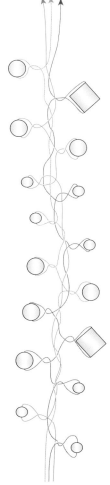

SIZE: 16" including clasp
MATERIALS:
Pink beads (6mm faceted crystals, 4mm clear crystals, 4mm milky crystals, 4mm iridescent crystals, 3mm pearls)
• Clasp • 26 gauge Pink wire
• Flat-nose pliers • Wire cutters

1. Start with 3 wires, each 36" long.

2. Twist wires together on one end.

3. String a bead or a group of beads and twist to form a short stem.

Repeat beading pattern in a random manner to the end. Alternate adding beads on different wires. Loosely braid wires together.

Add a clasp to each end.

Illusion Necklaces

Almost invisible necklace wires make floating beads around your neck quick and easy. Add small crimp beads on the wire to hold the beads in place for a beautiful look.

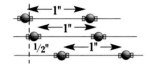

Necklace 1: Delicate Black Pearl

MATERIALS: Three 18" lengths of 0.25mm SuppleMax • 42 Black 4mm pearls • 90 Silver crimp beads • 2 Silver 6mm jump rings • Silver clasp

INSTRUCTIONS: On one strand, crimp a bead at one side of center and crimp 6 beads 1" apart on each end. On next strand begin at the other side of center, repeat. Begin ½" from the center on last strand, repeat to add 8 beads at each side. Attach clasp.

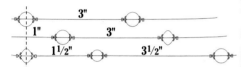

Necklace 2: Crystal & Pearl

MATERIALS: Three 18" lengths of 7 strand 0.51 Beadalon • 4 Pearl 10mm textured beads • 3 Crystal 10mm beads • 2 Crystal 8mm beads • 3 Crystal 10mm baroque beads • 24 Silver bead caps • 50 Silver crimp beads • 2 Silver clam shell end crimps • Silver clasp

INSTRUCTIONS: On top strand crimp a 10mm Crystal at the center, attach a 10mm textured bead 3" away at either side of the center bead. On center strand, crimp a 10mm textured bead 1" from the center, add a 10mm baroque bead 3" away at either side. On bottom strand, crimp a 10mm baroque bead at the center, add an 8mm Crystal bead 1½" at either side, then place a 10mm crystal bead 3½" away from the 8mm ones. Attach clasp.

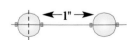

Necklace 3: Faceted Crystal 1 Strand

MATERIALS: 18" of 7 strand 0.25mm Beadalon • 11 Pale Gold 12mm faceted beads • 24 Silver crimp beads • Silver clasp

INSTRUCTIONS: Crimp a bead at the center. Add 5 beads 1" apart at either side of the center one. Attach clasp.

Necklace 4: Black Pearl 3 Strand

MATERIALS: Three 17" lengths of 7 strand 0.25mm Beadalon • 60 assorted Grey Baroque pearls • 3" of Black chain • Black clasp • 134 Black crimp beads • 2 Black 6mm jump rings

INSTRUCTIONS: Crimp a bead at the center of each strand. Place 10 beads 1" apart at either side the center one. Attach jump rings through end loops. Attach the chain at one end, attach clasp at the other end.

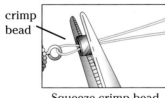

crimp bead

Squeeze crimp bead flat with pliers.

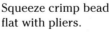

Make 3
Make 2
Make 2

Necklace 5: Pearl 10-Strand

MATERIALS: Ten 16" to 17" lengths of 0.25mm SuppleMax • 39 Crystal 2mm beads • 24 Pearl 2mm beads • 13 Crystal 6mm beads • 26 Pearl 6mm beads • 6 Pearl 8mm beads • 6 Crystal 8mm beads • 2 Silver bellcaps with a loop • 2 Silver 6mm jump rings • Silver clasp • Hypo-Tube Cement

INSTRUCTIONS: Float beads on threads with glue. Measure from the center of each bead. Top strand: Center a 6mm Crystal, add beads 1" apart. Strands 2, 3, & 4: Center a 2mm Crystal, add beads 1" apart. Strands 5 & 6: Place a 2mm Pearl ½" at either side of center, add beads 1" apart. Strand 7: Place an 8mm Pearl 1" at either side of center, add beads 2" apart. Strand 8: Place an 8mm Crystal 1" at either side of center, add beads 2" apart. Strands 9 & 10: Place a 6mm Pearl ½" at either side of center, add beads 1" apart. Glue all ends in the bellcaps. Attach jump rings and clasp.

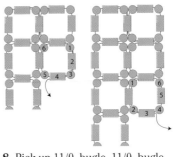

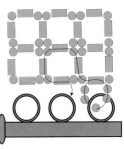

Squares Bracelet

Weave beads into a delicate net sure to catch compliments from all!

by Valarie Leland

MATERIALS:

Basic Supplies:
Three-strand slide bracelet clasp
Two size 10 or 12 beading needles
C-lon or Nymo B beading thread
Cosmetic sponge, optional

For the Bride...
Pearl Bracelet
5 grams 11/0 #123
5 grams #1 Bugle #123

Gray Bracelet
5 grams 11/0 #704
5 grams #1 Bugle #704

Red Bracelet
5 grams 11/0 #25C
5 grams #1 Bugle #25C

Notes: Work the center row first, using 2 needles. Then use one needle to complete each side and add the clasp. These instructions are for a 7.5" bracelet. Each row adds approximately one half inch to the length. Smaller adjustments can be made during attachment of the clasp.

A cosmetic sponge is handy to wrap the thread around and hold one needle while you use the other.

Start with 90" of thread. Thread a needle on each side about 20" from the end.

1. Pick up an 11/0 bugle, 11/0 bugle, 11/0 bugle, 14/0 bugle. Slide them to the center of the thread.

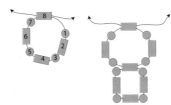

2. Pass the second needle in the opposite direction through the last bugle This is 'crossing the needles' through a bead. Pull to make a square and slide it to the center of the thread.

3. Pick up an 11/0, bugle,11/0 and bugle on the left needle. On the right needle pick up an 11/0, bugle and 11/0. Cross needles through the last bugle on the left side and pull snug. You now have 2 squares.

4. Repeat step 3 until you have a total of 28 squares.

5. Wrap the left needle and thread around a sponge or fold it inside a sticky note to keep it out of the way. Do not worry if the thread gets a little slack.

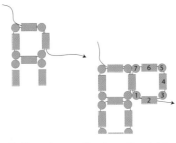

6. Pass the needle along the right side of the last square through the 11/0 and the bugle.

7. Pick up 11/0, bugle, 11/0, bugle, 11/0, bugle and 11/0 (beads 1 through 7).
Pass the needle down through the bugle on the center row and then through beads 1 and 2 of the current square.

8. Pick up 11/0, bugle, 11/0, bugle and 11/0 (beads 1 through 5). Go up through the bugle on the center row. Pick up an 11/0 (6) and go through the bugle on the square above this new one. Pass through beads 1 through 4 to get to the bottom of this new square.

9. Pick up an 11/0 (1) and pass the needle down through the bugle on the center row. Pick up an 11/0, bugle, 11/0, bugle and 11/0 (beads 2 through 6). Go through the bugle on the bottom of the square above this one and back through bead 1, the center bugle and beads 2 and 3.

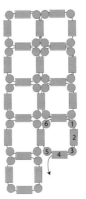

10. Pick up 11/0 seed, bugle, 11/0 seed, bugle, 11/0 seed, bugle (beads 1 to 5). Pass the needle up through the bugle on the center row. Pick up an 11/0seed (6) and go through the bugle on the bottom of the square above this one and then pass the needle through beads 1 to 4.

11. Repeat steps 8 and 9 until you have worked the length of the bracelet. Be sure not to take a 'shortcut' across a space with the thread. Always work around the squares to get your needle in position for the next stitch.

12. When you reach the opposite end of the bracelet, unwrap the left needle and wrap the right needle.

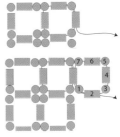

13. Flip your bracelet over and repeat steps 6 through 11 to complete the remaining row.

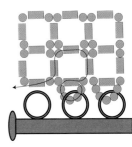

14. Pick up five 11/0 beads, thread the needle through the end loop of the clasp from back to front, then back through the bugle. Pass the needle back through these beads to reinforce.

15. Work the needle and thread through the squares as shown to the center row.

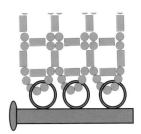

16. Pick up five 11/0 beads, thread the needle through the center loop of the clasp from front to back and then back through the bugle. Pass the needle back through these beads to reinforce.

17. Work the needle and thread around through the squares as shown to get to the last row.

18. Pick up five 11/0 beads, thread the needle through the end loop of the clasp from back to front and then back through the bugle. Pass the needle back through these beads to reinforce.

19. Work the needle through 2 or 3 of the squares toward the center of the bracelet and cut the thread close.

20. Unwrap the other needle and add the clasp by repeating steps 14 - 19. Make sure you have the clasp facing the correct way.